"As a pastor, I get asked lots of questions. I'm approached by unbelievers seeking to understand the gospel, new believers unsure about next steps, and maturing believers wanting help answering questions from their Christian family, friends, neighbors, or coworkers. It's in these moments that I wish I had a book to give them that was brief, answered their questions, and pointed them in the right direction for further study. Church Questions is a series that provides just that. Each booklet tackles one question in a biblical, brief, and practical manner. The series may be called Church Questions, but it could be called 'Church Answers.' I intend to pick these up by the dozens and give them away regularly. You should too."

Juan R. Sanchez, Senior Pastor, High Pointe Baptist Church, Austin, Texas

What If I'm Discouraged in My Evangelism?

Church Questions

What If I'm Discouraged in My Evangelism?

Isaac Adams

WHEATON, ILLINOIS

What If I'm Discouraged in My Evangelism?

Copyright © 2020 by 9Marks

Published by Crossway
   1300 Crescent Street
   Wheaton, Illinois 60187

Cover design: Jordan Singer

First printing 2020

Printed in the United States of America

Scripture quotations are from the ESV® Bible (The Holy Bible, English Standard Version®), copyright © 2001 by Crossway, a publishing ministry of Good News Publishers. Used by permission. All rights reserved.

All emphases in Scripture quotations have been added by the author.

Trade paperback ISBN: 978-1-4335-6820-6
ePub ISBN: 978-1-4335-6823-7
PDF ISBN: 978-1-4335-6821-3
Mobipocket ISBN: 978-1-4335-6822-0

Library of Congress Cataloging-in-Publication Data

Names: Adams, Isaac, 1989- author.
Title: What if I'm discouraged in my evangelism? / Isaac Adams.
Description: Wheaton : Crossway, 2020. | Series: Church questions
Identifiers: LCCN 2019025511 (print) | LCCN 2019025512 (ebook) | ISBN 9781433568206 (paperback) | ISBN 9781433568213 (pdf) | ISBN 9781433568220 (kindle edition) | ISBN 9781433568237 (epub)
Subjects: LCSH: Witness bearing (Christianity)
Classification: LCC BV4520 .A235 2020 (print) | LCC BV4520 (ebook) | DDC 269/.2—dc23
LC record available at https://lccn.loc.gov/2019025511
LC ebook record available at https://lccn.loc.gov/2019025512

Crossway is a publishing ministry of Good News Publishers.

BP		29	28	27	26	25	24	23	22	21	20
15	14	13	12	11	10	9	8	7	6	5	4	3	2	1

Who is sufficient for these things?

2 Corinthians 2:16

Such is the confidence that we have
through Christ toward God. Not
that we are sufficient in ourselves to
claim anything as coming from us,
but our sufficiency is from God.

2 Corinthians 3:4–5

A lion sat in front of me.

For years now, Sunday after Sunday, I've seen my pastor, Mark Dever, boldly declare the gospel and known his reputation as a faithful personal evangelist. Yes—*this* man was an evangelist. *This* man was a lion for the truth.

Until he wasn't.

One day, Mark shared with our church how he didn't feel so much like a *lion* evangelist but a *lousy* evangelist, at least in terms of his personal evangelism. He cited one encounter as proof.

On a flight, Mark wanted to share the gospel with the guy sitting next to him but hadn't had the opportunity, as his neighbor quickly put on his headphones. Standing at baggage claim after the flight, Mark and this man struck up a conversation. It took a turn Mark wasn't expecting when the man said, "Man, I'm so glad you're not one of those evangelical Jesus freaks. Have you ever been on a plane with them? Oh, it's *the worst*. There you are, you can't leave, and they just go on and on."

Mark thought about what to say—and then Mark said nothing. They got their luggage and parted ways.

Of course, Mark's silence could've been wisdom: "Answer not a fool according to his folly" (Prov. 26:4). But Mark confessed that wisdom didn't motivate him in that particular moment. Fear of man did.

Mark startled me with his humility. It takes a lot to use yourself as a negative example in public. I mean, this was *Mark Dever*. The man had literally written a book called *The Gospel and Personal Evangelism*!

Mark's story profoundly affected me. I didn't assume that "if he can't do it, there's no hope for me." Instead, I found myself in good company. If even my pastor faltered in evangelism from time to time, then there must be some hope for me.

What's Common to Us

Too often, I'm like Mark in that airport. And
if you've picked up this little book, my guess is
you are too. Maybe at one point in your life, you
told the gospel to anyone who might listen, but
you've felt that passion cool. Or maybe you're
eager to share the gospel with taxi drivers or
other folks you'll (in all likelihood) never see
again, but not so eager when it comes to sharing
the gospel with folks you see regularly.

Whatever it is, let Mark's example remind
you of the apostle Paul's words: "No temptation
has overtaken you that is not common to man"
(1 Cor. 10:13). In other words, you're not alone.

What's also common to Christians, however,
is our commitment to evangelize the lost. By
"evangelize," I mean sharing the gospel with
someone in hopes that they repent of their sins
and believe in Christ for salvation. Every Christian should engage in evangelism. The Bible
makes this point repeatedly:

- Matthew 28:18–20
- Mark 12:31
- Acts 1:8; 8:4; 11:19

- Romans 10:12–15
- 2 Corinthians 5:11–21
- Ephesians 4:15
- 1 Peter 3:15

In those passages, you'll find examples and instruction to share the gospel. Just to make sure we're talking about the same thing, here's what I mean when I use that word *gospel*. The gospel is the message that God is holy and people are not, but Jesus lived a perfect life, died on the cross, and was raised three days later for those who would turn from their sin and trust in him. In so doing, they receive the gift of eternal life.[1]

This book is for those who want to share that gospel message but, for whatever reason, struggle to do so faithfully. Perhaps you get awkward or silent when an opportunity to share the gospel emerges, or you feel like you don't live a good enough life to tell people about a good God. Maybe you don't want to lose a job or friendships. But following Christ means loving those who don't follow Jesus, and that love includes sharing the gospel.

What are some reasons you may not be sharing the gospel? Do you expect the church staff to do it or perhaps just the extroverts in the church? Are you too busy with your plans to think about someone else's eternal state? Are you a Christian in name but a Universalist in practice, acting as if God will simply save everyone in the end anyway? Are you ashamed of God's justice and goodness in judging and condemning sinners? If any of these reasons describe you and your lack of evangelism, I'd like to gently say two things:

First—you need to repent.

Second—there's hope for you.

If you're a discouraged evangelist, or if you feel like one, this book is for you. The good news for bad evangelists is that the same gospel we want to preach to others is the same gospel that gives us the power to obey Christ's command to share the gospel with others.

Understanding Our Job in Evangelism

How do you define success in evangelism? What makes a "good" evangelist? Many Christians assume that good evangelists are those who regularly see conversions from their evangelistic efforts, while bad evangelists don't see conversions. But according to Scripture, a bad evangelist is simply any Christian who doesn't regularly share the gospel—no matter the results. Now when I say "regularly," you may want to know how many people you should evangelize to be considered "regular." But the Bible doesn't give such a number and seeking one might reveal a wrong posture toward evangelism—treating it more like a chore to check off your spiritual to-do list than a privilege to enjoy.

Evangelism shouldn't be something we merely *have* to do; it's something we *get* to do. Evangelism may be our job, but it should primarily be our joy. Just consider: *God* has given *us* the ministry of reconciliation (2 Cor. 5:18). The King of kings has us as his messengers!

So instead of asking how many people you should evangelize each week, ask yourself: "Could I be described as someone who faithfully shares the gospel out of love for God and my neighbor?" We can be more or less faithful, but generally, how would you say you're doing?

Rightly understanding our job in evangelism is crucial because we easily get discouraged in evangelism *for the wrong reasons*. Discouragement is one of Satan's favorite arrows, and he loves to confuse and dishearten evangelists into silence.

You may be sharing the gospel faithfully but have yet to see someone actually believe. That's hard. But our job is to proclaim salvation not produce it. We're called to deliver a message to people; God's the one who delivers people from sin.

Imagine how odd it would be if a mailman was discouraged because he thought "Every time I deliver a letter and someone opens it, they don't like what they read!" It's not the mailman's job to make people *like* the mail but to *deliver* it. Likewise, it's our job to deliver the gospel to people, and God's job to cause them to believe the gospel. We share the faith, and God grants the faith. As Jesus said, "No one can come to me unless it is granted him by the Father" (John 6:65).

Our Joy & Job	God's Joy & Job
Sharing the gospel	Granting faith in the gospel

Too often, Christians are like *discouraged* mail carriers for the gospel. Is that you? If it is, let me encourage you to consider turning your attention from your evangelism to the character of God. Discouraged evangelists should hope in God. Why? Well, we have countless reasons, but the following nine reasons have particularly encouraged me. I pray they do the same for you.

What's Our Hope?

1) Hope in God Who Counts Us Righteous in Jesus

So, it happened again.

You clammed up.

You feared man.

You didn't share the gospel.

A pang of grief nags you. *Some evangelist I am.* But don't shoo this thought away too fast. After all, grief—good, godly grief—leads to repentance (2 Cor. 7:8–10). Yet the main reason we can repent is the main thing we often lose sight of: God's grace given to us in God's Son, Jesus. He is our hope before God.

Even if you've been sinfully silent in evangelism, take comfort from 1 John 2:1:

> My little children, I am writing these things to you so that you may not sin. But if anyone does sin, we have an advocate with the Father, Jesus Christ the righteous.

If you're a discouraged evangelist, remember this: *Jesus, not your evangelistic track record, is your righteousness before God.* Of course, we shouldn't use this truth as an excuse not to evangelize. We don't sin so that grace can abound (Rom. 6:1). Rather, those who've been freed from sin want to obey. We want to love Jesus. It's our love for Jesus and his love for us that motivates our evangelism (2 Cor. 5:14). Guilt may motivate you for a while, but that motivation won't last. However, knowing Jesus and the grace God has given you through him—enjoying him more than you do your career or yourself—will make you a faithful evangelist. Reflecting on God's grace will make you care more about what God thinks of you than what people think of you.

Sharing Jesus comes from the overflow of loving Jesus. This may surprise you to hear in a book on evangelism, *but evangelism isn't everything—Jesus is.* He's our Lord, yes, but he's also our brother, one who sympathizes with our weakness (Rom. 8:29; Heb. 4:15).

So relax.

Enjoy God's grace.

Enjoying God, it turns out, is a large part of what it means to obey God. Discouraged evangelists too often think they can be dutiful evangelists without being happy evangelists. Yet we shouldn't separate the two.

If you don't want to be a discouraged evangelist, fix your eyes on Jesus. Strive to enjoy him more. No grandparent has to be told to talk about their grandkids. Their delight in them bubbles over. While talking about grandchildren doesn't offend people the way talking about Jesus might, the principle holds true: the more we delight in Jesus, the more we'll share Jesus. As one author wrote, "Our power in drawing men to Christ springs chiefly from the fullness of our personal joy in Him, and the nearness of our personal communion with Him."[2]

What are some ways to reflect more deeply on the gospel and on the grace of Christ?

- Spend time meditating on God's word.
- Pray through passages of Scripture and ask God to impress on your heart a greater love for the gospel.
- Regularly attend your church and seek out discipling relationships with other saints.
- Read biblically faithful books that hold out the character of God and the promises of the gospel (you might consider starting with Tim Chester's excellent book *Enjoying God*[3]).

These are just a few suggestions. Ultimately, if you want to grow in evangelism, do all you can to fix your eyes on God's Son, our brother, Jesus.

2) Hope in God Who Blesses Us with Children

Family is a wonderful gift. The Bible regularly reminds us that a wife and children are gifts from the Lord (Ps. 127:3; Prov. 19:14). What's more, all Christians can enjoy the gift of family in the local church—brothers and sisters, mothers and fathers in the faith (1 Tim. 5:1–2). Just as family is for everyone, so is this section.

Writing to his son in the faith Timothy, the apostle Paul commended Timothy's family for faithfully sharing the gospel with Timothy.

> I am reminded of your sincere faith, a faith that dwelt first in your grandmother Lois and your mother Eunice and now, I am sure, dwells in you as well. . . . Continue in what you have learned and have firmly believed, knowing from whom you learned it and how from childhood you have been acquainted with the sacred writings. (2 Tim. 1:5; 3:14–15)

Don't miss this detail about Timothy: his grandma and mom spiritually influenced him. Timothy first heard the gospel from them. Never underestimate the spiritual value of raising your children in the fear of the Lord. *Parents, keep sharing the gospel with your kids. They are your primary gospel audience.*

And yet many Christian parents carry unnecessary guilt because, while they used to be regularly evangelizing their neighbors and discipling other Christians, now all they can seem to do is focus on the needs of their kids—*these exhausting kids*! After having children, many Christians feel as if they've been moved off the front lines, where "real" ministry happens.

But parents, you *are* on the front lines. Christian parents, the normal means of Christianity's advancement is through children being raised in the fear of the Lord. Families are to be schools of faith. God says so in the Old Testament:

> You shall teach [my words] to your children, talking of them when you are sitting in your house, and when you are walking by the way, and when you lie down, and when you rise. (Deut. 11:19)

And he says so in the New Testament:

> Fathers, do not provoke your children to anger, but bring them up in the discipline and instruction of the Lord. (Eph. 6:4)[4]

Scripture teaches that children matter for Christianity, and Christianity matters for children. I'm reminded of this truth each time my church hears testimonies from new members. At a recent members' meeting, twenty-six out of the thirty-two people who joined the church came to faith as kids. This proportion is not unusual and reflects a general pattern in my church and many others.

If you don't have kids, rejoice in the fact that you get to be on the front lines with the parents. God hasn't just given kids to the parents; he's given kids to your entire church. Who knows how God might use that flannelgraph you hold up as you volunteer in the children's Sunday school?

Friends, sharing the gospel with kids isn't only the parents' job. The entire church has the joy and responsibility of bringing up children under its care in the nurture and admonition of the Lord. So, the next time you hear a kid crying during the service, instead of getting annoyed, praise God for life in the church and for yet another opportunity to teach the gospel to a little one.

3) Hope in God Who Rules over Salvation

Parents, if you have adult children who aren't Christians, you know firsthand that raising children in a Christian home is no guarantee they'll love the Lord. But hear this clearly: if your kids don't love the Lord, that doesn't mean you did a bad job raising them.

A parent's sorrow over an unbelieving child echoes the perplexity we all feel when our evangelism yields no apparent fruit. So often, faithful evangelists are discouraged evangelists, aren't they?

But we're not alone in our discouragement. The fraternity of evangelistic fatigue has more members than we might think, and the apostle Paul was one of them.

If ever there was a discouraged evangelist, it was Paul. People rejected him. Paul probably wanted to leave his post at times. Yet consider what God said to Paul in Acts 18:9–10 in the midst of one of Paul's missionary journeys:

> Do not be afraid, but go on speaking and
> do not be silent, for I am with you and no

one will attack you to harm you, for I have
many in this city who are my people.

In other words, God told Paul to keep
preaching the gospel because the Lord had appointed people who would hear and believe
through Paul's teaching. Don't miss the echoes
of the Great Commission in Acts 18:9–10. Just
as Jesus told his followers, "I am with you" in
Matthew 28:20, so God reassured Paul, "I am
with you" in Acts 18:10.

And how did Paul respond?

Paul stayed a year and six months, teaching
the word of God among them. (Acts 18:11)

God's reassurance of his presence and sovereignty put steel in Paul's spine. His faith in God's
sovereignty produced evangelistic endurance.
Just as it did for Paul, God's sovereignty should
encourage us to continue evangelizing.

Remembering God's sovereignty in salvation is crucial to growing in evangelism. Many
Christians get discouraged in evangelism because they think that if they just used the right
technique *then* people would repent and believe.

Of course, the Bible commends evangelistic strategy and winsome presentation (see Paul's example in 1 Corinthians 9). How we relate to unbelievers does matter (2 Tim. 2:26; Titus 3:2; 1 Pet. 3:15). But ultimately, our hope isn't our method. Our hope is our God, and salvation belongs to him.

What Doesn't Save	Who Doesn't Save
Manipulation Smoke machines Perfectly crafted conversations Bells and whistles	You

What Saves	Who Saves
The gospel (Rom. 1:16; 1 Cor. 2:1–2)	God

God's sovereignty in salvation encouraged Paul to endure in proclaiming salvation. Paul knew *what* saved people and *who* saved people. He didn't trust in his eloquence or skill, in lofty speech or wisdom; he simply declared Christ and him crucified (1 Cor. 2:1–2). Paul trusted in the plain, old gospel because the gospel "is the power of God for salvation to everyone who believes" (Rom. 1:16).

Like Paul, we don't know who God has sovereignly appointed to believe in our cities and towns. Then again, that's kind of the point! Our job is to share the gospel broadly. In Mark 4:26–29, Jesus told a parable about the kingdom of God and said it's as if a man should scatter seed on the ground. The man sleeps and rises night and day, and the seed sprouts and grows, and the man *knows not how* (cf. Eccles. 11:5).

Take comfort and enjoy the freedom of this truth: God rules over his kingdom and those who are saved into it. We don't need to know all that God is doing; we just need to trust that he's the one doing it. And one day, we'll see God's wisdom and purposes vindicated, and we will know God was right all along.

4) Hope in God Who Vindicates His Justice

Sharing the gospel can often be frightening because we fear rejection. As we look through Scripture, we find that the apostles regularly faced rejection. In Acts 18, for instance, the Jews that heard Paul's message "opposed and reviled him" so intensely that he turned his attention to the Gentiles (v. 6). I wonder, if you were Paul in that moment, would you have thought to yourself, *Man, sharing the gospel with these people was a waste of time*?

I once shared the gospel with a friend who rejected it. As we parted ways, I felt like a failure and like I dishonored God. I see now, however, that my discouragement emerged from a misunderstanding. I was approaching evangelism like a salesman: I acted as if I had to sell the gospel to my friend, and since I didn't close the sale, I figured my boss (God) would be mad at me. And so, I was mad at myself.

But friends, being rejected for sharing the gospel is normal. Didn't Jesus tell us as much?

If the world hates you, know that it has hated me before it hated you. (John 15:18)

Instead of making us despair, rejection should make us rejoice. The apostles rejoiced when they got to suffer for Jesus's name (Acts 5:41). But they weren't always so bold. Not too long before they rejoiced in suffering, Jesus's disciples abandoned him (Mark 14:50). And too often, we're like the disciples: afraid of man and embarrassed of Christ. Nonetheless, though all forsook him, Jesus pressed on to the cross, to the grave, to the skies—for us, *despite* us. What a Savior!

Friends, the irony of our fear of man is that, if anything, Jesus should be embarrassed to be with us, not the other way around. But Jesus isn't reluctant to be with us. Instead, he gives grace to disciples who falter in fear (John 21:15–19). Heartened by this truth, let's be unashamed of the testimony about our Lord (2 Tim. 1:8). Let's not despair when rejected but instead rejoice.

Of course, just as Paul did, we still should feel deep sorrow *for people* who don't know Christ (Rom. 9:2). But Jesus taught in Luke 6:22–23 that we shouldn't feel sorrow *for ourselves* because those people may have rejected us—after all, people rejected Jesus and the prophets. Instead, we should "rejoice" because a great "reward" awaits us.

What Normally Happens
We're rejected.
↓
We forget God's promises.
↓
We despair.

What Should Happen
We're rejected.
↓
We remember God's promises.
↓
We rejoice.

If people didn't believe Jesus or the prophets, they won't believe us. If they mocked Jesus and the prophets, they'll mock us. People may even hurt us, just as they did Jesus and the prophets.

Just consider the tragedy that occurred in 2015 when an extremist Muslim group beheaded twenty-one Christians in Egypt. Later that year, a white supremacist murdered nine black people at Emmanuel A.M.E Church in South Carolina. Surely persecution is a reality we must consider.

Physical persecution is a frightening reality. Being persecuted with words—being maligned as Peter talks about in 1 Peter 2:12—is also scary. But we must be careful that fear doesn't lead us to disobey. We must not be like the Israelite spies who, when they saw the giants in Canaan, gave a bad report (Num. 13:32). No, we must continue giving the good report of the gospel. We should continue trusting in God's word and not fear man. As Jesus says,

> Do not fear those who kill the body but cannot kill the soul. Rather fear him who can destroy both soul and body in hell. (Matt. 10:28)

If you don't have a trail of souls you've won behind you, take heart: people rejected the prophets, the Lord, and the apostles. Yet the prophets, the Lord, and the apostles still glorified God in their ministries, and we can too.

We must never forget that God is glorified in the gospel going out regardless of the response. Even the rejection of his message serves to vindicate his justice on the last day. Those who have heard the gospel won't be able to say, "No one ever told me!" The Bible's storyline makes clear that God will save his people mightily and judge his enemies justly—and this truth should comfort Christians and lead us to praise God. The only time we see the word *Hallelujah* (which means "Praise the Lord") in the New Testament is in Revelation, and it comes in the context of his judgment:

> After this I heard what seemed to be the loud voice of a great multitude in heaven, crying out,
>
> > "Hallelujah!
> > Salvation and glory and power belong
> > to our God,
> > for his judgments are true and just;
> > for he has judged the great prostitute
> > who corrupted the earth with her
> > immorality,
> > and has avenged on her the blood of
> > his servants." (Rev. 19:1–2)

We praise God and tell others about God because he is just.

What's more, sharing the gospel, even if rejected, still bears witness that God is good, and he can be trusted. Even if nothing apparently happens to the *evangelized* after evangelism, the *evangelist* can still be built up in the faith having trusted God enough to testify about him.

Faithful evangelists trust God; faithless evangelists don't. As one author said, "God is as much, if not more, interested in doing a great work *in* us as he is in doing a great work *through* us."[5] God is at work *in* you even when it seems he's not working *through* you, and discouraged evangelists would do well to remember this.

5) Hope in God Who Gives Us Second Chances

Earlier we said that if ever there was a discouraged evangelist, it was Paul. Well, if ever there was a lousy evangelist, it was Jonah. God had charged him to preach to the city of Nineveh:

> Now the word of the LORD came to Jonah the son of Amittai, saying "Arise, go to Nineveh, that great city, and call out against it." (Jonah 1:1–2)

You may know how the story goes: Jonah disobeys and winds up in the belly of a fish where he eventually confesses, "Salvation belongs to the Lord" (Jonah 2:9). The fish spits Jonah up. And then what does God do with Jonah?

Does he give up on him? Scold him? Not quite. Consider Jonah 3:1–2:

> Then the word of the LORD came to Jonah *the second time*, saying, "Arise, go to Nineveh, that great city, and call out against it the message that I tell you."

God gives Jonah the same charge, which is to say, God gives Jonah a second chance.

Surely, I'm not the only evangelist in the world who would love a second chance at sharing the gospel with a family member, a neighbor, or a coworker.

God is so gracious that *sometimes* he grants a second chance. Time may need to pass before that second chance is given. We might need to rebuild some relational capital. But we serve a second-chance God. We should look for second chances in evangelistic conversations; we should pray for them. Don't let past evangelistic failures keep you out of the game.

Yet I fear some of us stay out of the game because we treat evangelism like a superpower—we either have it or we don't. This mentality is dangerous. Those who think they do have "the gift" get discouraged when they don't see immediate fruit from their ministry. Those who think they don't have "the gift" don't develop the discipline of evangelism and never get to work sharing the gospel. They treat evangelism as the kid on the next page treats playing the piano.

Evangelism is a discipline, and like any other discipline, we have to practice to grow in it. If we expect to be fluent with the gospel, but only evangelize every blue moon, we're like the person who expects to speak Spanish fluently after taking a few lessons.

We understand this principle when it comes to other spiritual disciplines. No one expects to understand the Bible perfectly the first time they read it. We have to read and re-read Scripture to grow in our understanding (Prov. 2:1–5; 2 Tim. 2:7). Likewise, with evangelism, we have to share and re-share to grow in our abilities.[6]

Yet here's hope: as long as you have breath, you have another chance to grow in sharing the gospel. So take God up on it. You never know what he might do.

6) Hope in God Who Delights to Use Weaklings

Jonah was a grumpy, reluctant evangelist. Nevertheless, the Lord brought him to Nineveh for his second chance.

And how did Jonah use it?

He offered what may be the most pathetic call to repentance in all of Scripture. We see it in Jonah 3:4:

> Jonah began to go into the city going a day's journey. And he called out, "Yet forty days, and Nineveh shall be overthrown."

That's it. No smoke and lights. No bridge diagram. Just a sentence! But look at what happens next:

> And the people of Nineveh *believed God*. They called for a fast and put on sackcloth, from the greatest of them to the least of them. (Jonah 3:5)

Jonah's wimpy sentence worked! Of course, this sentence is probably a summary of all he actually said. But this summary helps convey that what *Jonah* said isn't the main point. After all, notice who the people believed. They didn't believe *Jonah*, they believed *God*. Jonah was simply God's mouthpiece.[7]

If you've ever been a reluctant evangelist because you feel like your presentation isn't the best, take heart: God is the one who makes *his* appeal through us (2 Cor. 5:20). It's no wonder Paul would write:

> Not that we are sufficient in ourselves to claim anything as coming from us, but our sufficiency is *from God*. (2 Cor. 3:5)

Paul knew himself to be a weakling (2 Cor. 12:1–10). In fact, Scripture tells the story of many weaklings: Jonah pouted, Moses stuttered, Esther cowered, and the donkey God spoke through wasn't exactly known for its piety and erudition. We could go on, but the point is simple: God uses weaklings.

How might he use you?

Sometimes we don't evangelize because we simply don't believe God. We don't believe he'll save. We don't believe his word has power. But if God can speak through a reluctant prophet like Jonah, if he can speak through a stuttering shepherd in Egypt like Moses, and if he can speak through a donkey, he can make his appeal through you. This is the way of God—using what's weak to show his power (2 Cor. 4:7).

Hall of Weaklings as Seen in Scripture

Person	Passage	Used by God?
Moses	Exodus 4:11–12	Yes
Donkey	Numbers 22:21–39	Yes
Esther	Esther 4:14	Yes
Jonah	Jonah 1–4	Yes
Paul	2 Corinthians 12:1–10	Yes
You and Me	2 Timothy 3:16–17	?

As I've struggled to believe in God's power to save, one thing that's helped me is reading the testimonies of unlikely converts. Read the testimony of the apostle Paul, who ravaged the church (Acts 22:1–21; Phil. 3:1–14). Read the testimony of an English professor, Rosaria Butterfield, who you might have thought would never come to Christ, or read the testimony of Thomas Tarrants, a former ally of the KKK, and marvel at God's power to save.[8]

7) Hope in God Who Hears Our Prayers

In Ephesians 6:19–20, the apostle Paul asked for prayer—that he would have words to share the gospel and boldness in doing so. In Colossians 4:3–4, Paul asked for prayer—that he would speak the gospel clearly. I'm hard-pressed to think of something evangelists need more than boldness and clarity. And Paul asked for prayer *because he was confident God would answer*.

What about you?

Do you ask for God's help in your evangelism?

Do you ask others to pray for your evangelism?

Perhaps we have not boldness and clarity because we ask not for boldness and clarity.

Discouraged evangelists are prayerless evangelists. In other words, people who pray for people to come to Christ probably share the gospel. People who don't pray about it rarely share the gospel. One pastor noted, "The evil one has scored a great victory in getting sincere believers to waver in their conviction that prayer is necessary and powerful."[9]

Even in our prayerlessness, Jesus still intercedes for us. That's why Hebrews 4:16 exhorts us to draw near to the throne of grace with confidence, that we may receive mercy and grace to help in time of need. If you think it's just any old thing that the one who made the universe bends to hear your prayers, then this point will not comfort you. But if you think prayer is powerful, if you consider it a privilege, then this point will be a pillow for your soul. Faithful evangelists recognize that they need God's help.

So, very practically, think of someone you can share the gospel with this week.

Write the person's name here:

_____

Maybe you need a second chance with this person, as we talked about earlier. Maybe you need boldness or clarity. Whatever you need in your evangelism, take it to the Lord in prayer. If you're wondering what you might pray for or how you might pray, here are three suggestions:

- Thank God for being a good Father who knows what you need (Matt. 6:8).
- Pray for God to impress upon you the reality of heaven and hell to the point where your soul shakes.
- Pray to enjoy God more! Rev. Francis Grimké prayed "to be so thoroughly in love with [God] and thy work that I shall delight to speak of thee to others."[10]

Beloved, whatever your evangelistic need may be, *pray about it*. And then *talk about it* with someone in your church.

8) Hope in God Who Helps Us with the Local Church

Did you notice to whom Paul wrote those prayer requests in Ephesians 6 and Colossians 4? He wrote to local churches. Why does that matter? Because it shows that we don't have to go about our evangelism alone. We have the church. The local church can and should help us in our evangelism.

A friend who recently trusted in Christ told me that a woman in my church invited him to a Bible study where he heard one of the pastors teach. Meanwhile, another member of the church followed up with him after the service to discuss the lesson more. It wasn't just one person at work. The Lord used the work of the church to bring this person to faith. This group effort displays what my pastor calls "swarm evangelism."[11]

Brothers and sisters, evangelism is a team sport. A person's conversion is often preceded by hearing the gospel many times from many places. So we share the gospel with someone (the event of evangelism) and that person keeps hearing the gospel from others before conversion (the process of evangelism). Paul puts it like this in 1 Corinthians 3:6: "I planted, Apollos watered, but God gave the growth."

No one has a bird's-eye view on God's garden. Some of us plant, others water, *but God gives the growth*. So maybe you didn't get to share the full gospel with a coworker. But you've put a spiritual rock in their shoe—maybe that colleague is more open to Christianity than they were before they talked to you. *That's a win.* Someone else might come along and water that seed.[12]

Whatever your situation, don't lose hope about the seeds you've sown because there are other brothers and sisters who might reap. As one pastor put it: "The seed may lie under [the earth] till we lie there, *and then spring up*."[13]

You may be discouraged because you don't see fruit from your efforts. Perhaps that's because you're trying to calculate what you aren't meant to see. Friends, we can't calculate our own fruitfulness; that's God's arithmetic to do. Yet our hope is that as we work, serve, pray, and evangelize in the local church, God will produce fruit in a way that confounds our wisdom and displays his glory. God uses the ministry of the whole church to draw people to himself, not just our individual evangelistic efforts.

Take hope that God will use your efforts along with others. Faithfulness is all that's required of us. In Matthew 25, Jesus makes this point, and in verse 21 he extends a wonderful invitation to his faithful servants:

> Enter into the joy of your master.

We think about that joy in our last section.

9) Hope in God Who Rejoices in Heaven

In Luke 15, Jesus tells three stories about something lost being found and the joy that comes from finding it. He does this to illustrate the joy heaven has when one sinner repents (Luke 15:7). Brothers and sisters, heaven will be the happiest place because all of God's children will have been found (John 6:37).

We get tastes of heavenly joy in this life. As we see the Lord bless our evangelistic efforts, we taste heavenly joy when we see new converts baptized. We taste heavenly joy when God sustains us despite rejection. Maybe we even have the joy of leading someone to faith, being a midwife of the new birth. These are but appetizers to the joy we'll experience in heaven.

Yet when Christ returns, we'll enjoy *the full feast*, the marriage supper of the Lamb (Rev.

19:6–9). In heaven, God's joy will abound over the fruit of evangelistic seeds that we planted in good soil (Matt. 13:1–23).

So there may be hardship in our evangelism now, but there is joy ahead. Hang in there. God's got you, and he's holding you just as tightly *and joyfully* as he did when he first found you. With him, you can do this—*you can* share the gospel.

And he can bring the fruit.

After all, "with man this is impossible, *but with God all things are possible*" (Matt. 19:26).

Share the gospel. Tell someone that Jesus got up from the dead. Do it whether you're as lousy as Jonah or as faithful as Paul. As you do, hope in God. Paul prayed that the church in Rome would fulfill their ministry as they hoped in God:

> May the God of hope fill you with all joy and peace in believing, so that by the power of the Holy Spirit you may abound in hope. (Rom. 15:13)

I'm praying the same for you.

A Summary of the Gospel Confessed at Capitol Hill Baptist Church

The gospel is the joyous declaration that God is redeeming the world through Christ and that he commands everyone everywhere to turn from sin and trust Jesus Christ for salvation.

Each of us has sinned against God, breaking his law and rebelling against his rule, and the penalty for our sin is death and hell.

But because of his love, God sent his Son, Jesus, to live, for his people's sake, the perfect, obedient life God requires and to die on the cross in our place for our sin.

On the third day, Christ rose bodily from the grave and now reigns in heaven, offering forgiveness, righteousness, resurrection, and eternal blessedness in God's presence to everyone who repents of sin and trusts solely in him for salvation.

Recommended Resources

Mark Dever, *The Gospel and Personal Evangelism* (Wheaton, IL: Crossway, 2017).

Gregory Koukl, *A Game Plan for Discussing Your Christian Convictions* (Grand Rapids, MI: Zondervan, 2009).

Mack Stiles, *Evangelism: How the Whole Church Speaks of Jesus* (Wheaton, IL: Crossway, 2014).

Mack Stiles, *Marks of a Messenger: Knowing, Living, and Speaking the Gospel* (Downers Grove, IL: InterVarsity Press, 2010).

Notes

1. For a fuller summary of the gospel, see "A Summary of the Gospel Confessed at Capitol Hill Baptist Church" on pages 47–48 of this book.
2. Horatius Bonar, *Words to Winners of Souls* (Phillipsburg, PA: P&R, 1995), 13.
3. Tim Chester, *Enjoying God: Experience the Power and Love of God in Everyday Life* (Charlotte, NC: The Good Book Company, 2018).
4. While Ephesians 6:4 clearly calls fathers to spiritual leadership, we ought to remember that God also calls mothers to raise their children in the fear of the Lord. Consider Eunice and Lois, with whom we opened this section. I love their example because it shows that God can provide in the absence of a Christian father. We know from Acts that Timothy's father wasn't a Christian (Acts 16:1), and yet God provided for his faith. Though Paul was a spiritual father to Timothy (2 Tim. 1:2), Timothy's mother faithfully taught him from his youth (2 Tim. 3:15). Praise God for mothers who open their mouths with

wisdom and who have the teaching of kindness on their tongues (Prov. 31:26).

5. Mike Ayers, foreword to *The Pastor's Justification: Applying the Work of Christ in Your Life and Ministry* by Jared Wilson (Wheaton, IL: Crossway, 2013), 11.

6. Some folks talk about the "gift" of evangelism and may suggest the responsibility to evangelize only rests with those who have this gift, but this is an unbiblical conclusion. Evangelism is not listed in the lists of spiritual gifts in Scripture (though those lists aren't necessarily exhaustive). Nonetheless, the closest evidence for the "gift of evangelism" are evangelists God gives to local churches (Eph. 4:11). However, that seems to be more like an office in the church, and those evangelists are called to equip *the saints* for the work of ministry (Eph. 4:12).

7. For some of these observations, I am indebted to my friend Mack Stiles.

8. Rosaria Butterfield, *The Secret Thoughts of an Unlikely Convert: An English Professor's Journey into the Christian Faith* (Pittsburgh, PA: Crown and Covenant, 2012); Thomas Tarrants, *Consumed by Hate, Redeemed by Love: How a Violent Klansman Became a Champion of Racial Reconciliation* (Nashville, TN: Thomas Nelson, 2019).

9. Alistair Begg, *Made for His Pleasure: Ten Benchmarks of a Vital Faith* (Chicago: Moody Press, 1996), 50.

10. Francis J. Grimké, *Meditations on Preaching* (Madison, WI: Log College, 2018), 4.

11. For more on this point, see Mack Stiles, *Evangelism: How the Whole Church Speaks of Jesus* (Wheaton, IL: Crossway, 2014).

12. For practical advice on how to place spiritual rocks in shoes, see Gregory Koukl, *Tactics: A Game Plan for Discussing Your Christian Convictions* (Grand Rapids, MI: Zondervan, 2009).
13. Charles Bridges, *The Christian Ministry: With an Inquiry into the Causes of Its Inefficiency* (Carlisle, PA: Banner of Truth, 2006), 75.

Scripture Index

IX 9Marks

Building Healthy Churches

9Marks exists to equip church leaders with a biblical vision and practical resources for displaying God's glory to the nations through healthy churches.

To that end, we want to see churches characterized by these nine marks of health:

1. Expositional Preaching
2. Biblical Theology
3. A Biblical Understanding of the Gospel
4. A Biblical Understanding of Conversion
5. A Biblical Understanding of Evangelism
6. Biblical Church Membership
7. Biblical Chuch Discipline
8. Biblical Discipleship
9. Biblical Church Leadership

Find all our Crossway titles and other resources at 9Marks.org.

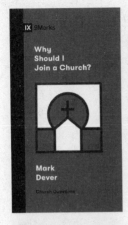